T0065516

Jerri Foster Schmidt

THAT FOSTER THING

STUDY GUIDE

GUIDING YOUNG WOMEN THROUGH THE GAME OF LOVE

WESTBOW
PRESS®
A DIVISION OF THOMAS NELSON
& ZONDERVAN

WestBow Press books may be ordered through booksellers or by contacting:

WestBow Press
A Division of Thomas Nelson & Zondervan
1663 Liberty Drive
Bloomington, IN 47403
www.westbowpress.com
844-714-3454

Because of the dynamic nature of the Internet, any web addresses or links contained in this book may have changed since publication and may no longer be valid. The views expressed in this work are solely those of the author and do not necessarily reflect the views of the publisher, and the publisher hereby disclaims any responsibility for them.

Any people depicted in stock imagery provided by Getty Images are models, and such images are being used for illustrative purposes only. Certain stock imagery © Getty Images.

Scriptures taken from the Holy Bible, New International Version®, NIV®. Copyright © 1973, 1978, 1984, 2011 by Biblica, Inc.™ Used by permission of Zondervan. All rights reserved worldwide. www.zondervan.com The "NIV" and "New International Version" are trademarks registered in the United States Patent and Trademark Office by Biblica, Inc.®

ISBN: 978-1-6642-2115-4 (sc)
ISBN: 978-1-6642-2116-1 (e)

Library of Congress Control Number: 2021901395

Print information available on the last page.

WestBow Press rev. date: 05/17/2021

Dedication

This book is lovingly dedicated to my six granddaughters: Mady, Maya, Charly, June, Georgia, and Hallie. They were my reason and inspiration when I wrote *That Foster Thing* and also now for this Study Guide. Their faces were ever on my mind and in my heart when I needed spurring on with this project. These darlings are featured in a photo on the back cover. Jiji loves all her girls.

To the girls and women who may in some way be helped by this book and its companion. May each one ultimately find hope and help in Jesus Christ.

To my Lord Jesus who got me through this endeavor for the furtherance of His kingdom. Come soon, Lord.

All Scripture Calligraphy

By

The author's granddaughter

Madyson Lynn Schmidt

Contents

Chapter 1   Viewing Ourselves...1

Chapter 2   Lying Lips..7

Chapter 3   Whatever Is Pure...13

Chapter 4   The Advocate...23

Chapter 5   Benefits of Wisdom..31

Chapter 6   A Higher Calling..39

Chapter 7   The Negatives...57

Chapter 8   Girls Know Girls...63

Chapter 9   Pursuing Excellence...69

Chapter 10   Forgiveness...79

Chapter 11   Where Is the Love?..87

Chapter 12   The Bigger Pic...95

Chapter 13   The X Factor..103

1

Viewing Ourselves

On page 3 of *That Foster Thing*, it says, "Another reason [we act the same as those without Christ] is we don't have a healthy view of ourselves." Let's explore what having a healthy view of ourselves would look like.

First of all, who are you?

You are the daughter of your mother and father. Write a sentence saying that, including your parents' names here:

_____

_____

_____

If you are a Christian, you are a child of the most high God.

The Bible says you are:

1. Chosen in Him

   For He chose us in Him before the creation of the world
   to be holy and blameless in His sight. (Ephesians 1:4)

2. Predestined to be His daughter

   In love, He predestined us for adoption to sonship
   [daughtership] through Jesus Christ, in accordance with
   His pleasure and will. (Ephesians 1:5)

3. Forgiven of sin

   In Him we have redemption through His blood, the
   forgiveness of sins, in accordance with the riches of
   God's grace. (Ephesians 1:7)

4. Bought at a price

   Do you not know that your bodies are temples of the
   Holy Spirit, who is in you, whom you have received
   from God? You are not your own; you were bought
   at a price. Therefore honor God with your bodies.
   (1 Corinthians 6:19–20)

5. God's handiwork

> For we are God's handiwork, created in Christ Jesus to do good works, which God prepared in advance for us to do. (Ephesians 2:10)

6. God's special possession

> But you are a chosen people, a royal priesthood, a holy nation, God's special possession, that you may declare the praises of Him who called you out of darkness into His wonderful light. (1 Peter 2:9)

Daughter of Him who sits on the throne

7. A coheir with Christ

> Now if we are children, then we are heirs—heirs of God and co-heirs with Christ, if indeed we share in His sufferings in order that we may also share in His glory. (Romans 8:17)

1. In light of what we just read that the Bible says we are in Christ, what would it mean to have a healthy view of yourself?

_____

_____

_____

_____

_____

_____

2. How do Christians, knowingly or unknowingly, look exactly like the world?

_____

_____

_____

_____

_____

_____

3. As believers we should act distinctively Christian in our daily lives. What would that look like for you personally?

_____

_____

_____

_____

_____

_____

2

Lying Lips

One of the most important things when choosing our friends is whether they are honest in character. On page 9 of *That Foster Thing*, I write of my desire to steer my daughter away from people who lie to their parents, teachers, or friends.

The Bible has some very direct things to say about speaking untruthfully.

There are six things the Lord hates seven that are detestable to Him:

1. haughty eyes,
2. a lying tongue,
3. hands that shed innocent blood,
4. a heart that devises wicked schemes,
5. feet that are quick to rush into evil,
6. a false witness who pours out lies,

7. and a person who stirs up conflict in the community.

(Proverbs 6:16–19)

In this passage of seven things the Lord hates, notice that lying is mentioned twice (vv. 17, 19).

It's also listed with murder (v. 17b). What a sobering realization that God hates lying so much that He groups it with taking a human life.

Proverbs 6:12–15, which leads up to the passage above, speaks of a "troublemaker and a villain who go about with a corrupt mouth." We can't assume that they are *only* liars, but we should want to steer clear of having any similarities with those who are characterized this way. I think we can put away any thoughts about lying being harmless after reading how God feels about it. Just a little white lie doesn't seem so small anymore, does it? Notice how in verses 13–14 this corrupt mouth then leads the body to "winking maliciously with his eye, signaling with his feet, he motions with his fingers, plots evil with deceit in his heart, he always stirs up conflict." Verse 15 then explains where this ends. "Therefore disaster will overtake him in an instant; he will suddenly be destroyed— without remedy."

To continue this thought, the Bible confirms this leading of the body with the tongue in James 3:6: "The tongue also is a fire, a world of evil among the parts of the body. It corrupts the whole body."

> I've heard it said that we're never more like the devil than when we're lying. In John 8:44 Jesus said, "You belong to your father, the devil, and you want to carry out your father's desires. He was a murderer from the beginning, not holding to the truth, for there is no truth in him. When he lies, he speaks his native language, for he is a liar and the father of lies."

These are scary words about lying. Hopefully, as Christians we will guard our tongues and speak the truth.

Now how can we apply what we've learned to where we are? Honestly ask yourself these questions.

1. How have I lied recently, and how did I or could I make it right?

_____

_____

_____

_____

_____

_____

2. What can I do to avoid situations where I'm tempted to stretch the truth?

_____

_____

_____

_____

_____

3. In what ways can I always avoid lying while still being kind to others?

_____

_____

_____

_____

_____

We've talked about what God hates. What makes God delighted?

> The Lord detests lying lips, but He delights in people who are trustworthy. (Proverbs 12:22)

We are students, and Jesus is our teacher. The student desires to become like his or her teacher. Therefore, we should study the Bible and pray to become like our master teacher. The Word says in Matthew 12:34b–35, "For the mouth speaks what the heart is full of. A good man brings good things out of the good stored up in him, and an evil man brings evil things out of the evil stored up in him."

Let's make it our practice to "hide God's word in [our] hearts that I might not sin against you" (Psalm 119:11).

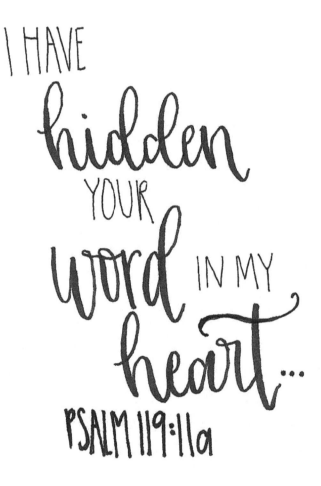

I HAVE *hidden* YOUR *word* IN MY *heart*... PSALM 119:11a

3

Whatever Is Pure

We're going to look specifically at two different parts of chapter 3 in *That Foster Thing*.

First, we'll discuss briefly the story of Joseph from Genesis 39. When you have a chance, read the whole chapter. We get into this story again in chapter 12 of this book. It will inspire you as you read how God blessed Joseph from the prison to the palace.

1. God blesses Potiphar through and because of Joseph (v. 1–6).

    From the time he put him in charge of his household and of all that he owned, the Lord blessed the household of the Egyptian [Potiphar] because of Joseph. (v. 5)

2. Potiphar's wife asks Joseph for sex, and he repeatedly refuses (vv. 6b–12).

> My master has withheld nothing from me except you,
> because you are his wife. How then could I do such
> a wicked thing and sin against God? And though she
> spoke to Joseph day after day, he refused to go to bed
> with her or even be with her. (vv. 9b–10)

3. Mrs. Potiphar accuses Joseph of rape unfoundedly and Potiphar throws him in prison, but God is still with Joseph (vv. 13–23).

> But while Joseph was there in the prison, the Lord was
> with him; he showed him kindness and granted him
> favor in the eyes of the prison warden. (vv. 20b–21)

Having God in our lives will help us every single day in every single way. Like Joseph, we will see that when God is with us, we can find favor in the most unexpected places!

Now let's get personal.

1. In what ways is God blessing your life?

_____

_____

_____

_____

2. How are you being tempted to sin?

_____

_____

_____

_____

_____

_____

3. How is your faith in Christ being challenged?

_____

_____

_____

_____

_____

_____

4. Describe how Christ has been with you in a tough situation.

_____

_____

_____

_____

_____

Now we will move on to the second part of chapter 3.

On page 14 of *That Foster Thing* we see Philippians 4:8. Let's look at it again along with verse 9. It says:

> Finally, brothers and sisters, whatever is true, whatever is noble, whatever is right, whatever is pure, whatever is lovely, whatever is admirable—if anything is excellent or praiseworthy—think about such things. Whatever you have learned or received or heard from me or seen in me—put it into practice. And the God of peace will be with you.

It looks like we've just read God's prescription for peace.

A lot of young people are anxious about many things. It is seen commonly in the older generation too. People are unnecessarily led into anxiety by what they see, hear, and read. This is how social media obsessions can deeply hurt our country. It's so important to be aware of what you allow into your mind. It can be critical to your thinking and your mental state.

Worrying over a bad grade is futile. If you've gotten a bad grade, study more and try harder going forward. If you're worried you might get one, use your energy to study instead of worry.

If you're worried about getting that promotion at your job, do the same as above. Prepare yourself to be a qualified candidate. If you were passed up for the promotion, leave it in the past and ask God for the right opportunity in the future.

Here are two good verses to memorize regarding worry. They happen to be in the Bible right before Philippians 4:8–9 (above):

> Do not be anxious about anything, but in every situation, by prayer and petition, with thanksgiving, present your requests to God. And the peace of God, which transcends all understanding, will guard your hearts and your minds in Christ Jesus. (Philippians 4:6–7)

DO NOT BE

anxious

ABOUT

anything.

PHIL 4:6a

These verses are loaded with so much great instruction and information. Also, the last time I checked, the word from verse 6 that says *anything* means *any thing*. God is telling us there is nothing, nothing, absolutely nothing to worry about. Just tell what's on your heart to God and leave it there. That means let it go. And then let the peace of God guard your heart and mind. Follow me?

Use your mind to meditate on the following (from Philippians 4:8–9):

Whatever is _____, not on what is false.

Whatever is _____, or of high moral quality.

Whatever is _____, not on what is wrong.

Whatever is _____, or free from sin or guilt.

Whatever is _____, not on what is unattractive.

Whatever is _____, or inspiring and deserving of praise.

Whatever is _____, not on what is average.

Whatever is _____, commendable, laudable.

Reading how someone thinks crudely of another on social media is not *any* of the above. The world likes to say that "your truth" and "my truth" is *truth*. That's bunk. (Not true). Someone's truth, if it is not an accurate description of reality, is not truth.

Let's say something that's true is said, but it's also hurtful and disrespectful. Well, those are reasons not to say it, write it, or even think it. It needs to pass the test of fulfilling all the "whatevers" of Philippians 4:8–9 to be put forth.

There used to be a sort of "meanness meter," as it were, when I was growing up, to do a checkup on yourself to determine whether you should say something out loud that you're thinking. It's in the form of three questions. They are, "Is it true, is it kind, and is it necessary?" If you'd take the time to ask yourself those three things, you might keep from saying it. You might also be: sparing someone's feelings, stopping before uttering something you'll regret, and avoiding having to go before the Lord in repentance, asking Him for forgiveness for running your mouth. On the other hand, if you get a "yes" for the answer to *all* three questions, then go ahead and say it. I think you'll find it will not be often when you can honestly answer yes to each of those.

Getting back to the Philippians passage brings out another reason I never wanted my kids to see horror movies or movies with bad, scary, or unsettling images. Those things are *not* pure, *not* lovely, and *not* praiseworthy. They can also cause interrupted peace and even nightmares.

So, if you desire God's peace, then think on the "whatevers" in Philippians 4:8 and follow by "putting it into practice" (verse 9)

1. What am I believing in my mind that is preventing me from experiencing God's peace?

    _____

    _____

    _____

    _____

    _____

2. Where could I change the "input" of my life to be free from my anxiety?

    _____

    _____

    _____

    _____

    _____

4

The Advocate

On page 21, in *That Foster Thing* we see about halfway down the page the following sentence: "Next, the most important issue in parenting is that the Holy Spirit is our unseen Helper when we can't see into the heart and mind of someone." It is also true that the Holy Spirit is the unseen Helper for all Christians because He is the third Person of the Holy Trinity. It is further true that we have an extremely limited view of the heart and mind of another person.

We're now going to look at some scriptures about the Holy Spirit of God. In John 14:15-19, 26-27 we read:

> If you love me, keep my commands. And I will ask the Father, and He will give you another Advocate to help you and be with you forever—The Spirit of truth. The world cannot accept Him, because it neither sees Him nor knows Him. But you know Him, for He lives with

you and will be in you. I will not leave you as orphans; I will come to you. Before long, the world will not see me anymore, but you will see me. Because I live, you also will live.

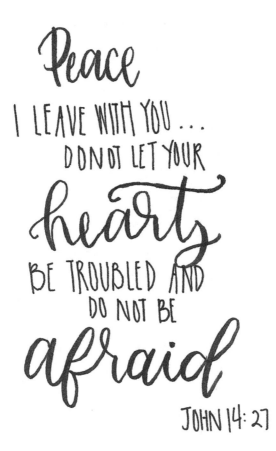

Peace
I LEAVE WITH YOU ...
D O NOT LET YOUR
heart
BE TROUBLED AND
DO NOT BE
afraid
JOHN 14: 27

And then verses 26 and 27 state:

> But the Advocate, the Holy Spirit, Whom the Father will send in my name, will teach you all things and will remind you of everything I have said to you. Peace I leave with you; my peace I give you. I do not give to you as the world gives. Do not let your hearts be troubled and do not be afraid.

Verse 15 is plain to understand, isn't it? If you love Jesus, then obey Him. If we say we love Him, but we don't do what His Word says for us to do, then who are we fooling? Ourselves? Certainly not Him. He knows if we love Him.

Have you ever heard the expression, "Talk is cheap?" If not, it just means that talking doesn't cost us anything. We can say we love someone, but the words carry no weight if we don't follow up those words with confirming actions. If we tell others that our Christianity is the most important thing to us, but we have no desire to go to church, study the Bible and pray, be with other Christians (His Church), help those in need, or witness to the lost world who will perish without Jesus, then our words mean nothing.

Now, we can't accomplish all these things, all the time, but there should be desire there and follow-up when possible. You can listen to what people say, but believe what they do. In other words, people's actions are who they truly are. Their words are empty. Believe what you see.

Remembering this will come in handy when trying to discern if someone could be a close friend for you. Friends who model Christlikeness are worth gold to a believer and help encourage us in our walk with the Lord.

Next, we see in verse 16 that Jesus says He will "ask the Father, and He will give you another Advocate to help you and be with you forever—the Spirit of Truth." My Bible footnote says this word *advocate* in the Greek means "one called alongside to help." How unbelievable is this? A Helper from God to be with me?

Then verse 17 says, "The world cannot accept Him, because it neither sees Him nor knows Him. But you know Him, for He lives with you and will be in you." This means that the Holy Spirit of God comes to live inside you. The world cannot accept this Spirit of the living God, nor will the world accept or understand this thinking. That's because the world of unbelievers does not know Christ.

Verse 26 says, "The Advocate, the Holy Spirit, Whom the Father will send in my name, will teach you all things and will remind you of everything I have said to you." This is very clear also. God our Father sends us His Advocate (Helper) to live inside us and to teach us and remind us of Jesus's words to His disciples (and by extension, to us). This means He will make clear spiritual things and the spiritual applications of physical things, both seen and heard.

I love these verses about the Holy Spirit. It is mind-boggling that God cares about us being "reminded of Jesus' words to us." He knows we need that. The last verse reads: "Peace I leave with you; my peace I give you. I do not give to you as the world gives. Do not let your hearts be troubled and do not be afraid."

All I can say here is, "Glory hallelujah!"

Can we grasp this? Read on to hear what we've been given. God sends us part of Himself to live inside us forever. This indwelling Spirit of God gives us peace. This is not worldly peace. He says He does not give to us as the world gives. What the world gives us is a one-size-fits-all kind of gift. It's not personal. If it is, it may or may not satisfy. If it does satisfy, then it will not last long. It will be very temporary. It might spoil or fade. Or maybe the worldly peace would not be ours to keep. The peace our Lord gives us is none of that worldly stuff.

Jesus is referring to heavenly peace. This is God's peace. Better than sleeping-baby peace. This is eternal, all encompassing, devil-defying, blood pressure lowering, and whole body, soul, and spirit peace. And then just to make sure we *get* it, He adds that we should not have troubled hearts or fear. No more lying awake at night worrying. Ask the Lord to take that away. John 14:27 says that I don't have to experience that. I have Him, inside me, to fill me, head to toe, with complete restful peace. What else can we find to worry about? I think the answer is supposed to be nothing. Nothing, nothing, absolutely nothing. He, our Savior, has taken care of everything. *Everything.*

The Holy Spirit will teach us everything and will never leave us.

1. How can I show the world that I love Jesus by obeying Him more?

   _____

   _____

   _____

   _____

   _____

2. How am I evidencing the reality of the Spirit of Truth living in me?

   _____

   _____

   _____

   _____

   _____

3. When have I experienced the Holy Spirit teaching me and/
    or reminding me of something Jesus has said?

    _____

    _____

    _____

    _____

    _____

4. Considering our Holy Spirit study on the previous pages,
    when we started this study guide of chapter 4, I referred to
    "not being able to see into the heart or mind of someone."
    How does the Holy Spirit help me discern whether a friend
    or possible date will be a good influence for me or someone
    I care about?

    _____

    _____

    _____

    _____

    _____

5

Benefits of Wisdom

In the last paragraph on page 26 of *That Foster Thing*, 1 Corinthians 15:33 is quoted. It says, "Do not be misled: Bad company corrupts good character." Honestly assess yourself. Are you drawn to bad influences for some reason? If so, recognize it as sin, and pray for God to remove that desire. Ask Him to replace them with Christian friends who truly care about living for Him. Ask a mentor to pray for you in this area if needed.

Proverbs 22:24–25 goes a little deeper with this same thought: "Do not make friends with a hot-tempered person, do not associate with one easily angered, or you may learn their ways and get yourself ensnared." Anytime there's a cautious word in the Bible, as this verse is, take a closer look. Usually there will be something you will want to avoid, or you may risk suffering the consequences. The word *ensnared* here is troubling. *Webster's Dictionary* defines *snare* as: "Anything dangerous, risky, etc. that tempts or attracts; thing by which a person is entangled; trap." In a nutshell, this means you can become like the angry person or trapped somehow when imitating that hostile behavior. Proverbs 29:22 expands the same idea. It says, "An angry person stirs up conflict, and a hot-tempered person commits many sins." Need we say more? It's yet another reason to avoid these hotheads. Many sins may be lurking around these individuals. For that reason, steer clear. That means, "Don't hang around to see if this person cools off. Get gone!"

Have you ever noticed firsthand the connection between being hot-tempered and many sins?

_____

_____

_____

_____

Walk
WITH THE WISE AND
BECOME
Wise
FOR A COMPANION OF
Fools SUFFERS
Harm.
PROV 13:20

Proverbs 13:20 points us in the right direction. It states: "Walk with the wise and become wise, for a companion of fools suffers harm."

How does walking with the wise make one wise or suffering harm come from being a friend of fools?

_____

_____

_____

This is a good directive, and these are words to live by. There is so much to learn about wisdom from the book of Proverbs. This book was written by King Solomon, son of King David. Solomon showed great interest in God's direction for God's people by asking the Lord for wisdom to lead them. He said in 1 Kings 3:9a: "So give your servant a discerning heart to govern your people and to distinguish between right and wrong." It would be a great prayer for us all—to ask God for a heart that could discern between these two paths. And maybe God would grant our request as he did for Solomon. The Bible says that the Lord was pleased that Solomon had asked for this, and He gave Solomon what he prayed for. First Kings 3:12 says, "I will do what you have asked. I will give you a wise and discerning heart, so that there will never have been anyone like you, nor will there ever be."

God said about Solomon, "There will never be anyone like you."

Let's scan some of the verses of 1 Kings 4 to see how wise God made Solomon. Verse 29 says, "God gave Solomon wisdom and very great insight, and a breadth of understanding as measureless as the sand on the seashore." Verse 30 says, "Solomon's wisdom was greater than the wisdom of all the people of the East, and greater than all the wisdom of Egypt." Verse 31 adds: "He was wiser than anyone else ... and his fame spread to all the surrounding nations." Then verse 34 says, "From all nations people came to listen to Solomon's wisdom, sent by all the kings of the world who had heard of his wisdom."

I think you get the idea loud and clear. Wisdom from God is unsurpassed. Never dismiss its value.

Proverbs 2:1–10 in the NIV provides an exercise for our wise benefit.

1. My son, if you _____ my _____, and store up my _____ within you,

2. turning your_____ to _____ and applying your _____ to _____,

3. indeed, if you call out for _____ and cry aloud for _____,

4. and if you look for it as for _____ and search for it as for _____ _____,

5. then you will_____ the _____ of the _____ and find the _____of _____.

6. For the _____ gives _____ from His _____ come_____ and _____.

7. He holds _____ in store for the _____, He is a _____ to those whose _____ is _____,

8. for He guards the _____ of the _____ and protects the _____ of His _____ _____.

9. Then you will understand what is _____ and
    _____ and _____—every good path.

10. For _____ will _____ your _____,
    and _____ will be _____ to
    your _____.

At the end of the first paragraph on page 26 of *That Foster Thing* someone is mentioned who is *set apart from the rest*. The text is referring to someone that you might be interested in dating. How could you tell if a guy would be a good person for you to date? First, and most important, is he a Christian? How do you know? Have you prayed and asked the Lord to lead you about this person? If so, how do you feel after praying? Have you asked your parents how they feel about it? If you're in college or vocation or away from your parents, do you have a trusted mentor that you can ask his or her opinion? How does this guy treat girls? How does he treat you? Does he put good effort into school and/or work/ activities/sports that he's involved in? Is he respectful of others? What are his parents and family like? How do you know? What kind of friends does he have?

Use the space below to answer the above questions about any date prospect. Once this space is filled, use a blank sheet of paper to answer these questions about any guy in the future with whom you want to consider spending your free time.

6

A Higher Calling

We're going to cover two different areas in chapter 6, with the first one being the longest.

At the top of page 31 of *That Foster Thing* I ask the following question: "Is what a Christian believes about alcohol consumption a hill to die on?"

I believe when it comes to matters of finding our life's partner, it just *may be*. Saying *it just may be* is me trying to say this with emphasis. "A hill to die on" is a military phrase referring to dying, or being willing to die, on a hill you're capturing as a soldier. I use this common old phrase for strong emphasis regarding the subject of alcohol, but we're not talking about actually dying here. It's *not* worth dying! Let's see what the Bible has to say on this subject.

There are several considerations regarding drinking alcohol. I will hereafter in these next few pages refer to this as just drinking.

First, there's the issue of minors drinking. According to Alcohol.org it is illegal in the United States at the time of this writing for people under the age of twenty-one to buy alcohol or consume it in public places. There is a gray area about the legality of minors' drinking depending on the presence of a parent, the state they live in, and also where the beverage is consumed. But for our purposes, we'll just subscribe to the most widely believed and enforced edict that drinking under twenty-one is illegal.

Alcohol.org also reports the following: "about 4,000 deaths per year are due to underage drinking." They also state that "it increases the risk for being involved in an accident, being victim of a crime, becoming injured & suffering from addiction later in life." Alcohol.com reports that "alcohol interferes with the way the brain regulates moods, impulses, and movement, and it disrupts normal thinking, decision-making, and memory functions. The brain is not fully developed in adolescence and introducing alcohol at a young age can lead to immediate potential hazards, and also to possible long-term damage and disruption of brain development."

I think we can safely say there is no good thing to come from underage drinking.

Let's move on to drunkenness. The Bible has some serious things to say about this subject.

Do not get drunk on wine, which leads to debauchery. (Ephesians 5:18a)

Nor thieves nor the greedy nor drunkards nor slanderers nor swindlers will inherit the kingdom of God. (1 Corinthians 6:10)

Do not join those who drink too much wine or gorge themselves on meat, for drunkards and gluttons become poor, and drowsiness clothes them in rags. (Proverbs 23:20–21)

Who has woe? Who has sorrow? Who has strife? Who has complaints? Who has needless bruises? Who has bloodshot eyes? Those who linger over wine, who go to sample bowls of mixed wine. Do not gaze at wine when it is red, when it sparkles in the cup, when it goes down smoothly! In the end it bites like a snake and poisons like a viper. Your eyes will see strange sights, and your mind will imagine confusing things. You will be like one sleeping on the high seas, lying on top of the rigging. "They hit me," you will say, "but I'm not hurt! They beat me, but I don't feel it! When will I wake up so I can find another drink?" (Proverbs 23:29–35)

The Ephesians verse above sums it up well. It leads to debauchery. According to *Webster's Dictionary*, some synonyms for debauchery are: corruption, depravity, immorality, iniquity, sin, etc.

We can further say that drunkenness leads to no good thing. Only sorrow.

Lastly there's the hot-button issue of Christians drinking any alcohol, period. Why is this controversial? It's disputed because you have Christians on opposing sides of the fence. Some say, "It's okay if you don't drink to excess. Many of the Bible characters we read about drank wine. The Word warns against being drunk but drinking in moderation is acceptable according to Scripture. Jesus Himself turned the water into wine in John chapter 2."

Then you have a smaller number of others who say, "Christians should not drink alcohol at all. It's a bad witness because it's a slippery slope into possible degradation." Also, you may hear, "The people who lived in Bible times did not have all the choices we have today for beverages. They may've had nothing else to drink." There's also a bit of a disconnect in what is reported about the actual alcohol content of the ancient wines as compared to today. Some say, "The wine of old that was commonly consumed was barely fermented. Even the beer of today would've been considered barbaric back then . They always drank wine that was heavily mixed with water." If that were true it would've taken a long time to get intoxicated in those days. The Bible admonition that warns against "lingering over wine" (drinking for a long time) seems to support that thought. This is all in contrast to our modern day with potent alcohol that causes inebriation much quicker.

To sum up, we just don't know for sure what the alcohol content was back then. We have good ideas, but there's always disputations as to the way things actually were. There are respected theologians on both sides. So, let's look at other aspects in the Bible.

Here are some things to consider.

1. You can be led astray by drinking.

    Proverbs 20:1 says, "Wine is a mocker and beer a brawler; whoever is led astray by them is not wise." If you can be led to an undesirable place by something, it means continuing in that direction is risky. This type of risky behavior is preventable.

2. There is an admonition against some biblical leaders drinking.

    Then [when Aaron and his sons became the first priests over Israel] the Lord said to Aaron, "You and your sons are not to drink wine or other fermented drink whenever you go into the tent of meeting, or you will die. This is a lasting ordinance for the generations to come, so that you can distinguish between the holy and the common, between the unclean and the clean, and so you can teach the Israelites all the decrees the Lord has given them through Moses." (Leviticus 10:8–11)

It is not for kings, Lemuel—it is not for kings to drink wine, nor for rulers to crave beer, lest they drink and forget what has been decreed, and deprive all the oppressed of their rights. (Proverbs 31:4–5)

Now see to it that you drink no wine or other fermented drink and that you do not eat anything unclean. You will become pregnant and have a son whose head is never to be touched by a razor because the boy is to be a Nazirite, dedicated to God from the womb. He will take the lead in delivering Israel from the hands of the Philistines. [Words of the angel of the Lord to the mother of Samson, a judge of Israel] (Judges 13:4–5)

But the angel said to him [to Zechariah, father of John the Baptist]: "Do not be afraid, Zechariah; your prayer has been heard. Your wife Elizabeth will bear you a son, and you are to call him John. He will be a joy and delight to you, and many will rejoice because of his birth, for he will be great in the sight of the Lord. He is never to take wine or other fermented drink, and he will be filled with the Holy Spirit even before he is born." (Luke 1:13–15)

We see there was a precedent in the Bible to abstain from wine for some who were set apart for leadership in God's kingdom.

3. A Christian's drinking can cause others to stumble.

> Therefore let us stop passing judgment on one another. Instead, make up your mind not to put any stumbling block or obstacle in the way of a brother or sister. I am convinced, being fully persuaded in the Lord Jesus, that nothing is unclean in itself. But if anyone regards something as unclean, then for that person it is unclean. If your brother or sister is distressed because of what you eat, you are no longer acting in love. Do not, by your eating, destroy someone for whom Christ died. (Romans 14:13–15)

Then skip down to verses 19–21.

> Let us therefore make every effort to do what leads to peace and to mutual edification. Do not destroy the work of God for the sake of food. All food is clean, but it is wrong for a person to eat anything that causes someone else to stumble. It is better not to eat meat or drink wine or to do anything else that will cause your brother or sister to fall.

This verse refers to the dietary laws of the Israelites that separated foods into clean and unclean categories. The main point to this passage refers to more than food as we can see (verse 21 in the last paragraph says, "or to do anything else that will cause your brother or sister to fall").

That's pretty straightforward talk. What you do affects others.

First Corinthians 6:12 says, "I have the right to do anything, you say—but not everything is beneficial. I have the right to do anything—but I will not be mastered by anything."

Drinking alcohol has an addicting quality. Drinking a little in the beginning most times leads to drinking much more as you get older. I heard a very wise quote one day. My dad, Hal Foster, said, "Many people say, 'I drink in moderation, and it hurts no one.' But sooner or later they fall on hard times, as everyone does during their lives. At those times, they will drink more than their moderate amount because alcohol has a numbing effect, and they think they can *handle* their lives better with a little more to drink."

This can hurt many people by this sad one losing the ability to think straight, act right, and drive sober. Also, he or she is at risk of influencing someone in his or her surroundings that will pick up the habit and maybe become an alcoholic because that person learned it from a beloved family member. Hard times in our lives have a way of lasting for seasons, not just a day here or there. After using the drink to numb one's pain from the hard knocks of life for a season, how many people have the capacity to go back to drinking just a little at isolated times? I would guess no one. The habit can easily reach the status of addiction in one's life. Not everyone succumbs to this, surely. But many do.

Many have thought drinking was cool, or harmless, but ended up hurt by it. Some people I loved were hurt by it. To take that a little further, could I hurt someone by my drinking? Of course. Who would I hurt from not drinking? No one. No one ever.

I feel called to help people, not hurt them. Help them see truth. Help them see Christ and thereby help them into His kingdom. We want to point people to our Lord by our words and our actions. Being different from the world in the area of drinking is one way we can do that. The overwhelming majority of people, including Christians, drink alcohol in some form sometimes. If we do not let our bodies be subjected to the powers of other substances like drugs and alcohol, maybe we can act sober and be a good example of someone who's led by the Spirit and not the flesh. That way, hopefully, we can be noticed for being different from the world in a good way. "Let your light shine before others, that they may see your good deeds and glorify your Father in heaven." (Matthew 5:16)

How do we sum this up as it relates to dating and marriage?

Your boyfriend's/fiancé's/husband's drinking will have a profound impact on you. My husband and I talk of how much we notice how a drinking partner has influence on the nondrinker in the relationship. If the couple stay together, then the nondrinker usually starts drinking also. Think about it. It would seem they would have to in order to have peace in the relationship. My mom used to say, "At least two drunks married to each other only mess up one household, and not two." Maybe they don't all mess up their homes and families, but many do. Again, it's the escalation factor. The dictionary defines escalate as, "to grow or increase rapidly, often to the point of becoming unmanageable."

My strong advice is don't date someone who drinks alcohol if you feel God has called you to abstain from it. That way you won't fall in love with a guy who is that different from you at the outset. Then you won't have to worry about compromising in the future on a behavior that you've felt wasn't the right path for you. Also, you could be sparing yourself some heartache from watching drunken behavior and maybe deteriorating health because of it, in someone you love. All the time you'd be knowing it didn't have to be this way.

1. Can you think of any case where it would be necessary for you to drink? If so, where and why?

   _____

   _____

   _____

   _____

   _____

   _____

   _____

2. How is drinking playing with fire?

   _____

   _____

   _____

   _____

   _____

   _____

3. What's the worst that could happen if you don't drink?

_____

_____

_____

_____

_____

_____

_____

4. What's the worst that could happen if you do?

_____

_____

_____

_____

_____

_____

_____

5. How is drinking making it "all about me" for a Christian?

_____

_____

_____

_____

_____

_____

6. What will you do if someone pressures you to drink?

_____

_____

_____

_____

_____

_____

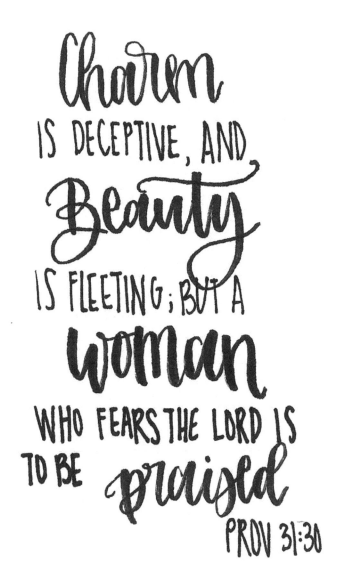

Charm IS DECEPTIVE, AND Beauty IS FLEETING; BUT A woman WHO FEARS THE LORD IS TO BE praised

PROV 31:30

For the second part of chapter 6 study guide, we go to pages 35 and 36 of *That Foster Thing* where we discuss how girls dress.

I Timothy 2:9a says, "I also want the women to dress modestly, with decency and propriety."

The motivation for choosing our outerwear points to our inner self. How, you ask?

Proverbs 31:30 says, "Charm is deceptive, and beauty is fleeting; but a woman who fears the Lord is to be praised."

Webster's Dictionary defines *charm* as any action or gesture assumed to have magic power, a quality or feature in someone or something that attracts or delights people.

Also from *Webster's*, we see that the word *deceptive* means deceiving or intended to deceive. *Deceive* means to make (a person) believe what is not true; delude; mislead. To be false to; betray.

The word *fleeting* (from *Webster's*) means passing swiftly; not lasting.

This basically says that the attraction (of this person) is not true (it's misleading); their beauty is passing swiftly. The rest of the verse is self-explanatory: "But a woman who fears the Lord is to be praised." The best quality in a girl or woman is her fear of the Lord. This phrase, "fear of the Lord," is used many times in scripture. *The Expository Dictionary of Bible Words* (Lawrence O. Richards, [1985], 272–73) says that in this sense it means "reverence for God. Fear of God is called the 'beginning of knowledge' in Proverbs 1:7."

"To fear God means to reject every competing deity" (all other gods) "and to serve Him only" (Deuteronomy 6:13).

"Fear of the Lord is expressed by walking in all His ways, by loving Him, and by serving Him with all our heart and soul." (Deuteronomy 10:12; Job 1:1; Psalm 128:1)

1. If my charms are deceptive, how can I be real when I'm getting to know someone?

_____

_____

_____

_____

_____

_____

2. If our outward beauty is going to fade away, how can we be inwardly beautiful?

_____

_____

_____

_____

_____

_____

3. Why do you think fearing the Lord is the beginning of wisdom? (Proverbs 1:7)

_____

_____

_____

_____

_____

_____

7

The Negatives

On page 38 of *That Foster Thing* we read: "The dating standards I'm proposing will be radically conservative compared to your daughter's peers, and for that reason, you have to control the negatives as much as possible. Oh, if we could only know where and who the big negatives were. Sometimes it will be obvious, sometimes not."

To me, the negatives are those things that you just don't feel good about. As the one being asked to go on the date, or as the one who is parenting/mentoring/helping this one, there's several ways to view the negatives.

It could be anything from an attitude to overt problem behavior and absolutely anything in between. You just have pause and concern about this person. Are these things that you can convince yourself are not a big deal? Do you want to let it go? More importantly, you've prayed a lot at this point about whether to encourage attention from this fellow or not. Is the Holy Spirit giving you the green light? If not, why not? Is it because the Lord is warning you of areas where you two are not compatible? If so, this point will increase in importance with each passing day.

So that's one aspect of the negatives I'm concerned about. The *big* negatives are next. These are people. A guy who makes us think he's someone he's not is a problem. This can be dangerous because it looks like he's dishonorable. If true, it means he's acting and trying to convince you and your family of a lie. Or it could not be that sinister at all. It could be that the person is just attracted to something about you, and he doesn't realize, or can't see, or doesn't want to see, that you two don't have that much in common. In that case he's not dishonorable, just not concerned about true compatibility.

Another big negative can be people on the periphery who are trying to encourage you to date someone that's not right for you. I'm guessing they don't take dating as seriously as I do. I've seen situations where the people encouraging the relationship are people in authority in this girl's life. Why would they encourage something that's doomed from the start? To be honest, I don't know the answer to this. Maybe they just love a love story? Maybe. Do they also love a breaking-up story? Surely not.

It should be noted also that different people have different opinions about the reasons for dating. Some date to have fun, some to have something to do, and some to get to know someone better that they think is special. I go with the latter. We've already stated that we know us humans can fall in love with anyone. *Anyone* could be a person as different from you as is possible. Romantic relationships have the power to bless a person's life to the maximum. Conversely, they can be the source of unsoothable heartache and suffering in life. Hence the reasoning behind choosing carefully with whom we go out.

I say, again, your standards may be radically different than your peers, and for that reason you must control the negatives as much as possible. If you do this, inevitably, you will feel pressure from those around you to ease up. Your friends may tell you that you have unreasonable expectations. That's something I can't speak to here. I *can* say that's something you pray about and get direction from God on. It's not that you're expecting perfection from anyone. You certainly don't want your date to expect perfection from you. What I'm trying to make completely clear here is that you control what you can by acting on the red flags if you see them. Why is that *so* important? Because you may get confusing messages from everyone else around you. Let God's voice in your heart be the *One* you listen to and act on. Let His voice be the loudest voice of all. Got it?

Bad
COMPANY
CORRUPTS
Good CHARACTER.

I COR 15:33b

1. What are the negatives that could surface in dating?

    _____

    _____

    _____

    _____

    _____

    _____

2. Again, we see 1 Corinthians 15:33, which says, "Do not be misled: 'Bad company corrupts good character.'" How have you/could you feel weaker in your walk with God around those with loose morals (impure lifestyles)?

    _____

    _____

    _____

    _____

    _____

    _____

8

Girls Know Girls

On page 45 of *That Foster Thing,* in the first paragraph we read, "We see ourselves in other girls. Sometimes, we see our worst self. In other words, we know we have the potential to act the same way." In this case we're referring to our make-believe situation with Demurely knowing exactly what Smoky is up to when she flirts with Dreamy. Can we just state the obvious here? Girls can be jealous, conniving, manipulative (of both guys and other girls), ruthless (showing no compassion), deceitful, and just plain ole mean. This list could actually be a lot longer. There's practically no limit to how low girls can go in their behavior. I say girls because I've seen all of this and more in girls, but not near as much pettiness in guys. Throw a dating relationship in the mix, and you'll see the fangs come out in some females. This is not just some girlish disagreement; this is about *my boyfriend.* Put another way, it's war.

Girls learn about boys when they're pretty young. Boys are still playing with planes and trains when girls are cluing in on how this whole thing works. Hence, they get possessive of boys sooner than boys do of girls. Their favorite childhood stories often include a Prince Charming. And this prince is usually seen rescuing a damsel in distress. Little girls watch this and think, "I want a prince too!" Boys see this same story and think, "I want a white horse." Isn't that funny? As you might expect, girls decide early what they want, and boys do too. Only thing is, they're not on the same page for years.

Girls want a prince. Boys want a horse.

When guys and girls get old enough to date, sometimes the girl has been dreaming of this for a long time. She wants to be the special one who gets rescued by the cute guy. Okay,

okay maybe she has a little bit of a fairy tale thing going on here. Nevertheless, having a boy pursue you is flattering for a girl. And once she's experienced this, she's probably going to encourage it and fight off the girl trolls who try to get his attention away from her. Notice the scary claws on this cute little kitten? Don't let her fool you. She knows what she wants, and she's not about to let it get away from her.

Thus far we've been establishing what girls want. Somewhere along the way this want can become a need. A misdefined need, that is. We're not talking about the basic human need for food, clothing, and shelter. We're referring to those who place way too much importance on immature romantic relationships. This is especially apparent in people who have not found their fulfillment in Christ to a point where they are willing to let Him direct their desires.

I don't want to fail to recognize our God-given desire for companionship in the opposite sex. That *is* a need. It's a need for the majority of mature adults. As we know, premating rituals are practiced and sought after among those who are not technically adults yet. What I hope to shed light on here is the obsession of immature people, especially girls, on "needing" a boyfriend. Out of this obsession can come this aggression toward other people, usually other girls, in a hostile pursuit of their possession. This possession is the guy. And by the way, she doesn't possess him. That's all an illusion. You don't "belong" to anyone until you get married. So, this is all way too premature.

Her need for this boyfriend can progress into her being needy for him at any cost. Sometimes the neediness is for the relationship, and not so much for this particular guy. That's when it's especially pathetic to watch. You can always tell she's just needy when she jumps quickly to another boy after things go off the rails with this one.

If your romantic relationship is meant to be, it will move slow and steady, not running down or demoralizing either person. It will also not usurp the importance of other God-given goals in your life. It will not control or dominate your time and will build up both persons. It will not tear down anyone, including people not involved in the relationship.

Each person—male or female—has the potential to be his or her worst self. Most girls can recognize immature Demurely and remember when they may've run the risk of acting just like her. Something held them back from stooping so low. Maybe it was their self-respect. Maybe it was the Holy Spirit helping them to refrain. With the Lord's help, we can strive for and pray to be led in His grace—not wanting harm for anyone and willing to wait for His best in His time.

1. What are some of the ways that neediness exhibits itself in romantic relationships and in relationships in general?

   _____

   _____

   _____

   _____

   _____

   _____

2. Why is neediness as a character trait something to suppress in ourselves?

   _____

   _____

   _____

   _____

   _____

   _____

3. How can neediness in our friends and boyfriends make the friendship challenging?

_____

_____

_____

_____

_____

_____

9

Pursuing Excellence

On page 53 of *That Foster Thing* we read, "I knew that striving for excellence and virtue was a noble and honorable goal worth pursuing for a lifetime." What does this mean? It means trying to be your best you. Trying to be your best you—for yourself, for others, but mostly for God.

What are the areas where God has gifted you? God's gifting can be a trait, characteristic, or ability in a certain area that makes things easier to do. It can be something you perform, play, exhibit, etc. It comes with an enlarged capacity for success and proficiency in doing it. You're extremely good at it, and people notice it. To observers you make it look easy. If you are not currently aware of what your strong suits are (areas where you succeed easily or somewhat easily) you would benefit from taking a survey on gifting to see where it leads you. The benefits of knowing how you are wired by God are substantial.

You will easily recognize when someone has a knack for something. The first sign is that other people either can't do it at all, or they can't do it unless they spend many hours a week doing it, practicing it, performing it, etc. And even then it probably won't have the flair of the one who does it easily. For the gifted one this could be an effortless mastering or easy mastering of something. Some examples could be: playing a musical instrument very well without much or any instruction, memorizing pages of text easily, speaking foreign languages proficiently without much studying, and photographic memory of things. Generally, people could describe what this gifted one can do as a genius level of achievement. It could be artistic talent that can't be taught or singing uncommonly on key and exquisitely beautiful. Maybe it's athleticism, and the body can do maneuvers on a court, arena, field, gym, swimming pool, golf course, etc. that make people's mouths drop open in astonishment. I don't mean to leave any particular thing out, because there is a world of things that people can be off the charts good at.

This is one type of gifting. Another one is the ability to do something, like maybe the talents listed above or one of the many things left off the list, but maybe not at genius level. You don't have to be a genius at something to still be gifted by God in this particular area. If you do it well without the normal struggles and time that it takes most people to excel at it, then you're probably blessed with a divine gift for it.

Where's this going? My point is: use it, develop it, practice it, work at it anyway. Be the best you can be. If you're already exceptionally good at something with little or no effort, what could you accomplish if you worked at it? There's no downside to putting your talents to good use for the purpose of glorifying God. Also, you would bless others by sharing your gifts. You might even cause someone else to praise God because of it.

1. Where are you gifted by God? What things come easy to you?

_____

_____

_____

_____

_____

_____

2. How could you share your gifts with others?

_____

_____

_____

_____

_____

_____

_____

The next subject in this chapter we will cover is in the area of baggage. On page 58 of *That Foster Thing* we see a cartoon of a fellow looking out his car window at all his luggage and belongings spilling out of his open trunk. The caption reads, "Baggage can be a lot to carry."

In chapter 7 of *That Foster Thing*, we touched on baggage and scars being the leftover effects of "dating around." What does this mean? It means in the area of relationships, people rarely come away from them without some lasting effects. For the good, not so good, or maybe even bad, we take with us things from our past. It's possible these are things people close to us have said to us, or about us, things they've done to us, and things we've felt. It may be things we've held on to in our memories for good or for ill.

Dating around is basically dating a lot of people. Your diligence to date smart will hopefully pay off. That payoff would hopefully be that the list of people you dated is small. A small list is the goal in my mind. The smaller the list, the less baggage you'll probably carry from it in the future.

A scar is a mark left on the body from a wound or injury. A wound probably needs no clarification. But just to leave no doubt, a wound is where a person has been hurt. This can be physical, mental, or emotional hurt. There's been pain associated with this scar, and it has left its mark.

Wounds in relationships can be from a multitude of things. Scars from past relationships are mostly memories of the above. I say *mostly* because you could have a physical scar from a wound where someone has physically hurt you. That's extremely serious and should be reported to the proper authorities. Never willingly be around someone who has physically injured you on purpose. I would say the same thing about someone wounding you emotionally. When you realize your friend or boyfriend is a bully, get out of the relationship.

Most times it's someone saying something about never forgiving you, never wanting you again, or never loving you. It can be what they said you inflicted on them. You may be told you made them feel unwanted, ashamed, or unloved. It's being told you are a disappointment to someone. It could be having your flaws exposed or your appearance unappreciated or ridiculed. It could be your efforts at something were laughed at, and your diligence was scoffed at. It could be something relayed to you that you did, said, or were. Or not. This means it could be untrue as to your fault in the matter. It could all be lies. It could've been spread around as gossip, and others may've weighed in on their hurtful opinions of you. It could be your most embarrassing moments laid bare.

Usually it's the people we care about or trust the most who have the potential to hurt us the deepest. Do you see why this is called baggage? It's those things we carry with us. One of the main reasons for this study is to help you be so careful who you let into this inner circle of people closest to you. These will be your closest relationships—your best friends, your dates, your boyfriend. Be careful, dear daughter, sister, friend. Do your homework in finding out the most you can about your best friends beforehand. From these will possibly come friends for life, an endearing boyfriend, or your future husband.

Don't let your hurt keep you from your best life.

If you do have hurtful scars and baggage, dear one, know that God is bigger than all of it. He has big arms to hug you, big shoulders to lean on, listening ears, a forgiving heart, and a redemptive plan for you. You don't have to live where your pain resides. He has forgiveness for you and through you to the offenders. Don't let your hurt keep you from your best life for Him. Lay it all at the foot of the cross. And leave it there, dear one.

1. Have you ever been hurt so deeply by someone that you can't seem to forget it? If so, can you lay it before the Lord for Him to put a healing balm on? Will you truly leave it with Him as much as it is in your ability to do, with His help? Use these lines to recall baggage in your life or not. You may share with your group or keep personal between you and the Lord.

_____

_____

_____

_____

_____

_____

_____

_____

_____

_____

_____

2. What could be some of the side effects of baggage?

_____

_____

_____

_____

_____

_____

_____

_____

10

Forgiveness

In chapter 10 of *That Foster Thing*, we had a short lapse from studying about romantic relationships before marriage and went into forgiveness inside of marriage. We looked at the power of forgiveness to sustain a marriage and possibly prevent divorce.

There may be no more important practice in marriage to keep it thriving over the long haul than this one thing. I felt compelled to touch on this because it might make or break your own marriage one day.

Very few people know how hard marriage can be before they say "I do." Once married, they see how tough it can be to stay in harmony with their spouse. Christian marriages are really no different than the general population when it comes to troubled unions and the sad event of divorce. That's why I wanted to include this one-word directive: "Forgive."

Ruth Bell Graham, the wife of well-known evangelist Billy Graham, once said, "A happy marriage is the union of two great forgivers." I say a heart-felt "Amen" to Ruth's wisdom! And I must add the following: If Ruth and Billy Graham, being one of the most prolific preaching and teaching couples for the kingdom of heaven to have ever lived, share this about forgiveness, it means that probably everyone on the planet will need this advice! If Ruth and Billy had to learn this, then we *all* will.

We could ask this question: Why is it so hard to forgive in marriage? I'm not sure why except that it probably has something to do with the fact that Satan doesn't want us to forgive or be forgiven. You see, we are never more like our heavenly Father than when we forgive those who hurt us. Also, forgiving one another is a powerful thing, as we talked about in chapter 10 of the book. It can make your physical body actually sick when you refuse to do it, and on the flip side, health could possibly be restored when you give in and do it. There's definitely a correlation between the mind, emotions, and body. Each of these aspects of a person affect the other aspects within the same person. Satan is going to fight us on forgiving others because he doesn't like unity and peace between people. Forgiveness brings restoration, and that's always a good thing.

If forgiveness will work for married folks, it will work for unmarried ones. So, let's expand our discussion about the beauty of it to the population in general. Forgiveness is needed by everyone, for everyone. And I don't mean that in a collective sense as much as in an individual manner. Each one forgiving another, and that one extending this kindness to the next one. You see, our God has forgiven us our sins, and that's how we get to be *His* child. If He's done that for us, how can we withhold it from anyone else? We forgive, because God forgave us. Simple, really. Simple concept but not easy to do. Just know you'll have an inner fight on your hands once you decide to be like your Lord. There can be great revival ahead if we listen to the Holy Spirit's still, small voice. Pray and ask Him for the strength to forgive. He will do it through you.

Let's do a Bible search to see what it has to say about this important Christian attribute called forgiveness. Scriptures are from the NIV.

1. This is what you are to say to Joseph: I ask you to
   _____ your _____ the _____ and
   the _____ they committed in treating you so badly.
   (Genesis 50:17a)

2. If my _____, who are called by my _____, will
   _____ themselves and _____ and _____
   my face and _____ from their _____
   _____, then I will hear from _____, and I
   will _____ their _____ and will _____ their
   land. (2 Chronicles 7:14)

3. For the sake of your _____ Lord, _____ my
   _____, though it is great. (Psalm 25:11)

4. Help us _____ our _____, for the _____ of
   your name; _____ us and _____ our _____
   for your name's sake. (Psalm 79:9)

5. And _____ us our _____, as we also have
   _____ our debtors. (Matthew 6:12)

6. For if you _____ other people when they _____
   against you, your _____ _____ will also

_____ you. But if you do not _____ others

their _____, your _____ will not _____

your sins. (Matthew 6:14–15)

7. Then Peter came to _____ and asked, "Lord, how

    many times shall I _____ my brother or sister who

    _____ against me? Up to _____ times? _____

    answered, "I tell you, not _____ _____, but

    _____-_____ times." (Matthew 18:21–22)

8. And when you stand _____, if you hold

    _____ against _____, _____

    them so that your _____ in _____ may

    _____ you your sins. (Mark 11:25)

9. Bear with each other and _____ one

    another if any of you has a _____ against

    _____. _____ as the Lord _____

    you. (Colossians 3:13)

10. If we _____ our _____, He is _____ and

    _____ and will _____ us our _____ and

    _____ us from all unrighteousness. (1 John 1:9)

11. In _____ we have _____ through His

    _____, the _____ of _____, in

    accordance with the _____ of _____ _____

    (Ephesians 1:7)

12. The Lord is _____ to _____, abounding in _____ and _____ _____ and _____. (Numbers 14:18a)

13. Be _____ and _____ to one another, _____ each other, just as in _____ God _____ you. (Ephesians 4:32)

11

Where Is the Love?

"Most people want love that just works. You know when it does, and you know when it doesn't." We see the preceding on page 72 of *That Foster Thing*. What does that mean exactly? I think it means the majority of people want to be in a relationship that is somewhat easy. Easy on their eyes (really cute to me), easy on their wallet (doesn't try to get me to break my budget), easy on their car (please don't wreck it), easy on their schedule (doesn't try to keep me from other important stuff frequently), etc. But none of these "easys" speak to the most critical one in my book. That would be easy on my emotions.

I would not want a romantic relationship, or any other kind, for that matter, that causes me pain and suffering. That would be the opposite of "easy" as described above. For example, dealing with a boyfriend who gives me emotional whiplash would be the worst of all dating experiences. His care and tenderness one day and his anger and volatility the next is not a good combination. It speaks to emotional problems in the guy. Steer clear of getting involved with anyone like that.

So how do we have one of these *easy* relationships? After all of our diligence to narrow in on that guy who meets our standards talked about earlier, what else do we need? Good question. A profound answer follows. He needs to have an interest in me. And I need to have an interest in him. You think? Absolutely this is mandatory. He may be like many guys who are great, but they just aren't my type. And I'm not their type, for whatever reasons. We already established that he needs to be above the fray and not the norm. But that's not enough. He needs to also be pursuing me. We need to be connecting in some way that shows both of us that there's *something* there. God, in His Sovereignty, has already brought him in my life in some capacity. So, what next?

While we're waiting on the Lord to bring this special guy into our lives, we concentrate on growing in the attributes that characterize a godly woman. If we want to find the right one, we need to *be* the right one. How can we be the right one? I think one way is to study what the Bible teaches about love and start showing love to others. Jesus said in John 13:35: "By this everyone will know that you are my disciples, if you love one another." Pray for God to help you develop this very important trait. Let's look at some Bible verses on love.

Love is patient, love is kind. It does not envy, it does not boast, it is not proud. It does not dishonor others, it is not self-seeking, it is not easily angered, it keeps no record of wrongs. Love does not delight in evil but rejoices with the truth. It always protects, always trusts, always hopes, always perseveres. Love never fails. (1 Corinthians 13:4–8a)

Said another way (by using the definitions of the attributes): love can accept or tolerate delays, and it is warm and generous. Love is not discontented or resentful, longing to have someone else's possessions or qualities, and it does not talk with excessive pride about one's own achievements or feel deep pleasure because of one's own accomplishments. It does not shame others or have concern for one's own welfare before others; it is not easily annoyed or hostile, and it doesn't keep a list of all the ways others have wronged them. Love does not delight in immorality or wickedness but shows great delight with the truth. At all times it keeps others safe from harm; it always believes in the reliability of someone, always expects the best, and always continues even in the face of difficulty. Love is never unsuccessful in achieving its goal.

ABOVE ALL,

Love

EACH OTHER
DEEPLY BECAUSE

Love

COVERS OVER A MULTITUDE
OF SINS.
1 PETER 4:8

A few more scriptures are especially helpful when you have disagreements or disappointments with your steady guy. First Peter 4:8 says, "Above all, love each other deeply, because love covers over a multitude of sins." Proverbs 10:12 says it a little bit differently with the same idea: "Hatred stirs up conflict, but love covers over all wrongs." The Bible always encourages us to go beyond what would be the average person's reaction. In the MacArthur Study Bible NIV footnote on this verse, he says, "We should always be ready to forgive insults and unkindnesses."

A good way to end this section is with another great verse—one from Paul to the church at Ephesus. Ephesians 4:2 says, "Be completely humble and gentle; be patient, bearing with one another in love." Can we say, "Amen"?

1. Name examples of how you could live out the qualities of love from 1 Corinthians 13:4–8.

   _____

   _____

   _____

   _____

   _____

   _____

2. How have you forgiven insults and unkindnesses that were directed your way?

   _____

   _____

   _____

   _____

   _____

   _____

3. Can you recall a time when you were able to "bear with someone (maybe someone being annoying) in love?"

_____

_____

_____

_____

_____

_____

12

The Bigger Pic

At the bottom of page 79 of *That Foster Thing* we return to the story of Joseph in Genesis. This time we are seeing the beautiful reunion of him with his brothers who had wronged him in his early years. In Genesis 50:18–20 we read:

> His brothers then came and threw themselves down before him, "We are your slaves," they said. But Joseph said to them, "Don't be afraid. Am I in the place of God? You intended to harm me, but God intended it for good to accomplish what is now being done, the saving of many lives."

Joseph forgave his brothers.

Joseph said to his brothers, "You intended to harm me, but God intended it for good," in speaking of the pain that Joseph was subjected to. He is referring to the fact that he was sold by his older brothers to traveling merchants on their way to Egypt when Joseph was only seventeen years old and living in Israel. Genesis chapter 37 details this story. We saw in our study guide of chapter 3 that Joseph ends up in prison at the hand of Potiphar, one of Pharaoh's officials. He is taken out of prison to interpret Pharaoh's dreams about the years of abundance and famine that the whole area will soon experience (Genesis 41:14, 29–31). Joseph wisely explains to Pharaoh how to conserve and manage the abundance to spare Egypt from ruin during the coming famine. Pharaoh realizes how valuable Joseph's plan is and says, "Since God has made all this known to you, there is no one so discerning and wise as you. You shall be in charge of my palace, and all my people are to submit to your orders" (Genesis 41:39–40a).

Life unfolded just as Pharaoh's dreams had foretold. In Genesis 41:53–56 we read:

> The seven years of abundance in Egypt came to an end, and the seven years of famine began, just as Joseph had said. There was famine in all the other lands, but in the whole land of Egypt there was food. When all Egypt began to feel the famine, the people cried to Pharaoh for food. Then Pharaoh told all the Egyptians, "Go to Joseph and do what he tells you." When the famine had spread over the whole country, Joseph opened all the storehouses and sold grain to the Egyptians, for the famine was severe throughout Egypt.

Apparently, the famine spread far and wide. As the next verse tells us: "And all the world came to Egypt to buy grain from Joseph, because the famine was severe everywhere" (Genesis 41:57). This is plain talk. God used Joseph in Egypt to prepare for the famine and then to facilitate the process of feeding all the starving people.

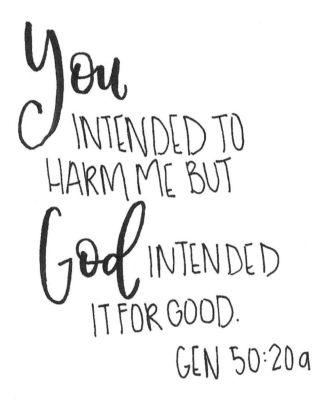

You intended to harm me but God intended it for good.

GEN 50:20a

This story has a great ending, but that's not the best or the most memorable part of it. If we look back in the first paragraph at our verses from the last chapter of Genesis we see in Genesis 50:20 where Joseph said to his brothers: "to accomplish what is now being done, the saving of many lives." And that's exactly what was happening. Many lives were being saved through Joseph's care and administration. The best thing is that Joseph realized his Lord's care and providence in bringing him to Egypt. Joseph tells his brothers: "But God sent me ahead of you to preserve for you a remnant on earth and to save your lives by a great deliverance. So then, it was not you who sent me here, but God" (Genesis 45:7–8a). This is such a clear picture of how God orchestrated the events in Joseph's life to bring him, his family, and truly this whole part of the ancient world to this shining moment.

God saw to it to bring Joseph out of his country and into another. He was with Joseph throughout all the happenings in his life, including being sold as a slave and later ending up in the palace prison through no fault of his own. God gave him the wisdom to foretell Pharaoh's dreams as a lowly prisoner. Then through the miracle of it all, he becomes second to Pharaoh in the whole land. He *did* save many lives. Better said, God saved these lives through Joseph. The point is that Joseph saw it. He saw God's deliverance. He saw God's sovereignty. Joseph got it. He saw the bigger picture.

It's really beneficial if we can step back from what's going on in our lives and say, "What is God doing in my situation? Wonder how God will use this tough, seemingly impossible set of circumstances for my good? Or someone else's good?"

Joseph chose to look at the hard things in his past and see that God was with him, and he was never alone. God equipped him through the hardship and prepared him to lead a whole country. Lives were saved. Lives were blessed. And God got the glory.

God in His sovereignty is leading, protecting, and orchestrating your life too, my dear one. Take comfort in this. You can rest and not worry because of it.

1. How has God shown you that He is handling all the details in your life from the small ones to the difficult ones?

_____

_____

_____

_____

_____

_____

2. How am I struggling to gain perspective so I can see the bigger picture in my life? You may have trouble seeing it until you're on the other side of whatever the troublesome areas are. Or it may even be years later.

_____

_____

_____

_____

_____

_____

_____

3. Am I concentrating too much on what I think I want and not seeing how God's will for me might be different? Can I let go to let God handle it?

_____

_____

_____

_____

_____

_____

13

The X Factor

What is the X factor? If I were to describe it, I'd say, you can't. Describe it, that is. You can try, but it's hard to do. It's something that's so rare, so unique and unexplainable, that you have trouble putting your finger on it. In dating it's that feeling, and attention-grab that just "gets" you. It's arresting. That means it makes you take notice of it. It can leave you without words. It's unforgettable. And all of this is in a particularly good way, of course.

Maybe, in reality, it's just that your attraction to this person makes you feel this way. Anyone who's ever dated more than a couple of people and found the X factor in someone knows exactly what this is. I say that, because if you've only dated one person, you have nothing to compare this experience to. You might get confused as to the true like-mindedness you may or may not share with your date. It would be possible to get wrapped up in the dating dynamic at first and not realize that you may be infatuated with that and not so much with the guy. Time will tell.

Again, the X factor is very hard to pinpoint. It is usually about what you feel. When a relationship is new, this "feeling" is hard to get out of your mind. It makes all the other dating you did seem very mundane and unremarkable. Your dating past becomes forgettable. At this point, it doesn't matter about any of your previous romantic relationships. This one is the only one that matters to you now.

People have tried to describe this phenomenon and have written books and, of course, love songs about it. It can make people forget things they shouldn't and be distracted about everything. It can make you silly and giddy.

She's got a way about her.

To explain further, I'd say the X factor is confirmed when you realize the other person is feeling the same way about you. If the X factor is experienced by both people, it makes the excitement build and validates your notion that this one is different than the others. Finding this one person who you are feeling so strong about becomes nothing special if it fizzles out in a short time. Also, if one party feels this way but the other doesn't, the relationship is going nowhere because it's not shared.

Having the X factor doesn't mean you'll have a perfect experience every time you're together. Nor does it mean that you will not have issues to work through. You may, in fact, have significant obstacles that present themselves. There may even be arguing that's sometimes hurtful. Our sinful human condition makes these scenarios more common than not. I would say, however, that a constant disunity and not seeing eye to eye more than the opposite could negate the existence of the X factor altogether. Either it will strongly motivate toward unity or it was never there after all. Most of the time this lack of harmony does not indicate that these two people have not found something extraordinary in each other. It just means that they'll have plenty of reasons to let God be their Guide to making peace with each other.

There may even be relationships that are so agreed upon between the two as to their authenticity that both parties are willing to argue and forgive and repeat that again and again because they can't give the other one up. Arguing about the same thing over and over may be the way it plays out. This can indicate an impasse because of their separately held positions. Is it a deal breaker? Does it threaten the life of the relationship? It depends on what the disagreement is about. Is it central to who one of them is? Are his or her firmly held core beliefs being discounted by the other? Do they see their futures not coinciding? These are tough questions that should be discussed and prayed about with the greatest consideration. If the X factor is there, the couple will probably decide to agree to disagree or just take their chances and stay together because the "magic" in their relationship is just too good to let go.

They know deep down that God has brought this one to them, and they want to make it work. God can teach us so much about grace and forgiveness through this pivotal relationship. Our love for and from this critical person motivates us to strive for understanding and bearing with one another. Arguing and forgiving with your soul mate usually makes the relationship even sweeter. Because now you know the other one's heart a little better than you did before the argument. And you love the person even more for it. There are relationships that are worth fighting for, and you'll know in your heart of hearts if this is one. God will see to it that you know.

1. On page 91 of *That Foster Thing*, middle paragraph, we talk about people delaying or not breaking up with someone they know is not right for them because they're being nice. How is this the opposite of being nice?

   _____

   _____

   _____

   _____

   _____

   _____

2. Marriage is hard. It will take you *and* God to make it work with your husband. It's been said that you shouldn't just marry someone you can live with but only marry the one you can't live without! I say you need both. Why is this true?

   _____

   _____

   _____

   _____

_____

_____

3. I end the book with a line from Billy Joel's song

    She's Got a Way. It goes like this:

    She has a way of pleasin'

    I don't know what it is

    But there doesn't have to be a reason

    Anyway

Why do the reasons that she is pleasin' not matter when the X factor is present?

_____

_____

_____

_____

_____

_____

Printed in the United States
by Baker & Taylor Publisher Services